A Message from a Blue Heart

Tony Moreno

Publisher contact information:
Book Writer Corner
433 Walnut Ct Pittsburgh PA 15237, USA
e-mail: info@bookwritercorner.com
https://bookwritercorner.com/
412-274-7334
ISBN: Paperback: 978-1-960815-70-5
Hardcover: 978-1-960815-69-9

Notice to the Reader: Concepts, principles, techniques, and
opinions presented in this manual are provided as possible
considerations. The application, use, or adoption of any
concepts, principles, techniques, or opinions contained in this
manual are the risk of the individual or organization who
makes that decision. The authors or their heirs or beneficiaries
shall not be held liable or responsible for any application, use,
or adoption of any part of this manual.

DEDICATION

This book is dedicated to my brother and sister law enforcement professionals everywhere, police officers, sheriff deputies, probation, parole, corrections, prosecutors, and all of our dedicated support staff who are just as important.

This book is dedicated to first responders, educators, medical personnel, counselors, youth coaches, mentors, caretakers, and other members of the community who selflessly contribute their time and effort to make our world a better place.

To Ryan, Kim, Desiree, Marcus, Aura, Adam, David, and Kimberly B. … Nolan, Shane, Alana, Kayla, Kieran, Meara, Frankie, Sophia, Cooper, Makenzie and Lennon … along with all of your future siblings and cousins.

And to all of our brave heroes and innocent little angels who are no longer with us. You are not forgotten.

CONTENTS

PREFACE

"Those who tell stories rule the world."
— **Plato**

I have been providing information and conducting training to law enforcement officers, civic groups, private organizations, citizens, and other members of the community since 1982.

With all of the people I have met and the places I have traveled, a few quotes and messages have impacted me to the point I wish to pass them on to others.

I also have words and thoughts that I use in my training that come from inside me and are inspired by the people I have met and the situations I have experienced.

I have written this book with the following objectives in mind …

To make you think about what you do
To help you understand what you do
To help you appreciate what you do
And to help you enjoy what you do

No one expects you to be a superhero. Simply respect and honor yourself, the people you serve, and your profession. If you do that, there will always be help to get you up off the ground.

The words in this book come to you from a lifelong member of the "thin blue line" and a "street cop" with a "solid blue heart."

You may not agree with some of my words or messages, but if there are one or two thoughts that you take away from this book and use, my effort to contribute is worthwhile.

No one can guarantee your safety, but your knowledge, instincts, attitude, physical conditioning, emotional stability, training, expertise, resources, and tactics can only bring the odds of being safe and successful into your favor. That's the best we can do.

Keep working on your odds …

ACKNOWLEDGMENTS

There are people who have made this book possible through their personal and professional support, honesty, influence, loyalty, and friendship over the years...

Nelson Arriaga, Dave Avila, David Avila Jr, Al Balderas, Aaron Brittingham, Darlene Burge, Yolanda Bybee, Wayne Caffey, Dennis Conte, Adam Friedman, Colleen Grosso, Clay Hodson, Rick and Suzy Logue, Wes McBride, Al McGilvray, Anthony Moreno, Aurora Moreno (mom), Tony Moreno Sr. (dad), George Norris, Nora Perez, Bob Ruchhoft, Natalie Salazar, Edwin Santana, Ted Spicer, Joe Suarez, Dave Wentworth

And to …

The California Gang Investigators Association (CGIA), Gang Cop International LLC, International Latino Gang Investigators Association (ILGIA), Los Angeles Police Department, Los Angeles Police Protective League (LAPPL), Police and Fire Publishing and Book Writer Corner.

Cover Design – Dylan Brittingham

Chapter 1
The Job

"You can never be great at anything unless you love it."
—**Maya Angelou**

It's Not How Much You Do; It's What You Do.

I learned as a young police officer not to "spin my wheels." In other words, you can be as busy as hell, but is anything important being accomplished? Do you do memorable things? Things that last in your mind and in the mind of others. Do you make a difference to somebody?

Here's an example

I used to interview gang members that were in custody in the LA County Jail to identify them and talk to them about what was going on in the gang world. I was working alongside the LA County Sheriff's Operation Safe Streets deputies, who at the time had an office in the jail. They were kind enough to give me a desk and allow me to work alongside them. I was focusing on gang members from the city of Los Angeles.

This operation worked so well that I expanded it to Sybil Brand Institute, which was the women's jail also controlled by LA County Sheriffs. I would go there one day a week and interview female gang members and other inmates.

One day a deputy told me an inmate wanted to speak to me and brought her into the interview room. The inmate had been arrested for prostitution and was to be released in two days. She said she could solve a murder if I agreed to help her out.

This inmate was only 20 years old and seemed pretty frightened. She was from another part of California, far away from Los Angeles. She left home and came to Los Angeles looking for a job and maybe hoping to catch a dream as a movie star while she was still young.

She ran into a pimp and was no match for his game and salesmanship. In no time, she was turning tricks for him and totally under his control. She had been threatened and abused and couldn't leave out of fear. Then she got arrested.

She was serving a short jail term, and when released, the pimp would be waiting outside the jail to scoop her up and put her back to working on the street. Meanwhile, her mother made arrangements to drive her back home, but she didn't think the pimp was going to let that happen. She needed help.

She gave me information on the murder, and that turned out to be solid, solving a "whodunit" type of homicide. Two days later, when she was to be released, my partner and I showed up along with the pimp. As she was being released, we detained him "conducting a prostitution investigation," making sure that he couldn't follow or catch up to her and her mom. She was free.

I don't know what happened to her, but I do remember that it was one of those moments that made me feel I had done something worthwhile. It didn't show up in the newspapers, count as a felony arrest on our recap, or even result in a citizen's letter of commendation, but in my heart, I knew we had done something very important.

That, to me, was worth more than a handful of mediocre arrests some officers seem to thrive on. I will always remember that day, and hopefully, in your career, you'll have enough of them to keep you going just like it did for me.

I felt very important on that day.

The More You Know, The Less People Lie.

If you're doing things right in your career, you should be getting better and better as time goes on. The job is all about communication and how you deal with people.

If you show respect, you're more likely to get respect in return. It's not a gang or gang culture thing; it's a people thing. The only difference is with a gang member disrespect can get a person killed right on the spot.

Also, with gang members, suspects, and/or criminals, a certain amount of respect comes across as self-confidence on your part. If you display a certain level of self-confidence, it tells whoever you're dealing with that you know your job, you understand the area you work in, and you can probably take care of yourself.

Criminals tend to feel that the average cop is pretty much a "square" who can be lied to because they lack the street instincts to know when they are being hoodwinked. It may be in your conversation, your body language, or how you generally carry yourself, but if the person you are dealing with believes that you know your stuff, they will tend to lie less.

Knowledge First ... Expertise Second

I have never been to Tahiti, but if you would like me to, I can make a darn good two-hour presentation on Tahiti tomorrow in front of a crowd and get paid for it. I can surf the Internet tonight and put together a presentation by morning. Although I might be entertaining, that wouldn't make me an "expert" on Tahiti. Well, maybe it makes me a "paper expert."

There are people out there who can go from first base to third without ever touching second in the area of expertise because it benefits them to be recognized as an "expert." It may bring notoriety, praise, and financial reward. But it doesn't mean you actually know the subject.

Take the time to gather information, develop it, and

before you know it, you'll be a "true expert." Work on having a solid base of knowledge that no one can ever take from you. There may be times when you aren't allowed or able to utilize your knowledge, but even if it's on hold for a while, you won't lose it. You may have to sharpen your skills at times, but it will always be there.

It may seem that the world is blowing up crime-wise all around you, but nothing much is going on where you work. That's when you take the time to prepare, work to get more knowledgeable, and be ready when the "big one" hits. When that time comes, you'll be better prepared to be the "go-to" person. That is what separates a true expert from a paper expert. Your expertise is a byproduct of your knowledge and experience. Make it solid.

Don't Be Fancy … Master the Basics.

I know officers that look good, sound good and make great first impressions, but to assess their actual value as law enforcement officers, they're "more frosting than cake."

I know other officers who are not so flashy, so brash, or so narcissistic but who are solid cops. The difference is discovered beneath the surface when you find out who they really are and what they really do.

As a young officer, I would always check out what other officers were doing and how they were doing it. I would see qualities in other officers that totally impressed me. I would also see traits in some other officers that had me scratching my head, and not in a good way. In trying to make myself a solid street cop, there were basic qualities in the cops that I admired and hoped to emulate.

Here are a few of the basics.

The good cops were leaders. It wasn't a matter of rank, but as situations developed and occurred in the street, the leader would emerge and take control. That officer would do it because he was courageous and could make decisions, and it was usually the best thing to do. He cared about his fellow officers and was not ego-driven. He was also very respected by his peers.

The best cops were motivated and usually motivated themselves. They didn't need all conditions to be perfect to effectively do their job. They wouldn't go out of their way to look for obstacles to slow them down and never made excuses for themselves.

The good ones were knowledgeable and knew how to develop information to constantly become even more knowledgeable. They were information magnets and used that information to increase their knowledge, and the more they knew, the better they were at getting information. The more information they received, the better they became. They created a positive cycle for themselves.

They used their knowledge and shared it. When you use information effectively, you increase your value and competency. When you share information, you make those around you better at what they do.

The best officers are tactically sound and can be counted on to be at their best in stressful situations. They are the fellow officers you want around when things happen and who instill confidence and the "warrior spirit" in those around them.

When it comes to police/community relations, the best officers realize the importance of making key relationships with members of the community. It really boils down to how an officer talks to and treats people. Some of the best officers weren't really warm and fuzzy as individuals, but they were decent enough to draw the respect of the people they came into contact with. They weren't more important than their job.

And finally, the best cops I saw knew how to manage themselves. They usually had other things in their lives besides police work and took their job and its responsibilities seriously, but they didn't take themselves too seriously. This allowed them to actually enjoy the job. That quality is extremely important as when it seems the entire world is attacking law enforcement, figuratively and literally, that officer is not shaken or thrown off course by negativity. He has a solid base.

Know the basics and master them. It's hard work, but it's the key to a long and rewarding career and life.

A Good Hitter Focuses on The Pitch, Not the Crowd. A Good Cop Does the Same Thing.

With all of the negative energy swirling around law enforcement nowadays, it's easy to get down and lose the hunger we all had when we were young puppies starting out in the battle between good and bad.

In Southern California, it seemed as though there was always some type of controversy or issue going on with law enforcement. So, in a way, it became a part of the life of a police officer.

It forced me to learn how to block out the distractions and issues that might affect some law enforcement officers but didn't directly affect me.

I understood I could be one citizen contact, one tactical situation, or one bad decision (in the media's eyes) from appearing on the front page of the Los Angeles Times or on the evening news. I was aware of that fact, but determined to keep that in the back of my mind and do my duty without that fear making me uneasy or creating any self-doubt.

If you have ever played baseball or softball, you know that when you are batting, you are so focused on the pitcher and the pitch coming at you that you block out all other distractions like the sound of the crowd, the gravity of the situation, or the runners on the move. Any of those things can distract you from the objective of hitting the ball.

Working in law enforcement, there are many things that can interfere with your focus on the job if you allow it.

You may have a sick child at home, a difficult case coming up in court, or are in the process of losing a relationship, but there are times when all that must be put aside.

When pulling a traffic violator over to issue a citation, approaching the front door on a radio call, or walking down the tier in a correctional facility housing violent gang member, the focus must be on what you are doing. All of your senses must be in tune with the goal you are trying to accomplish. I believe you can practice and sharpen that skill of focusing on the task at hand.

In fact, there were times when I enjoyed being at work because it allowed me an escape from things bothering me in my personal life. I could always trust my mind to block out distractions and focus on work.

At the present time, many current and former law enforcement officers believe things are so bad that no one can do any work. Yet, great arrests are still being made, great cases are being prosecuted, and many citizens have good experiences with law enforcement.

The suicide rate among cops was high 25 years ago, and it still is now. Divorce rates are traditionally high with law enforcement officers, along with PTSD, medical issues, and mental stressors. It boils down to the power of your mind and the control of perception, and of course, training your mind how to focus.

In Police Work, Not Everything Is Right or Wrong, Good or Bad, Black or White. There Are Many Shades of Gray.

As a young officer, I was under the impression most things were right or wrong. I had life experience, but becoming a police officer meant my mission in life was to right the wrongs in the world. I think most young officers feel the same way from an idealistic point of view.

What I learned along the way was in a world I believed was filled with extremes, not everything was that simple.

Everything doesn't always have to be "this or that" or "one or the other." Not everything necessitates choosing a side.

The best analogy is utilizing the colors black and white. I'm not referring to racial issues when I say black and white. Police work, as in life itself, falls into a gray area and is not necessarily the extreme polar opposites of black and white. Most decisions require an officer to use his or her logic, discretion, and/or decision-making abilities to resolve a situation. Sometimes the answer is not obvious.

The victim is not always truthful, the witness is not always accurate, and/or the suspect is not always lying. How well you navigate in the gray area may determine how successful the resolution to the problem will be.

The best officers keep an open mind, do not jump to conclusions, and deal with people and circumstances as individual situations. That is how you successfully navigate the "gray area" of your work.

I guess you can say that there are probably at least "50 shades of gray" in police work with or without the handcuffs.

Being a cop is like coaching. Everybody can do a better job, but no one ever does

I've been around sports my entire life, and as I have gotten older, I notice that a lot of fans like to criticize the players and coaches. It's like that in most sports, and it seems the fans get more spoiled and more critical, taking for granted the skill, effort, talent, and intelligence it takes to be successful at high levels of competition.

I was at a hockey game and had to suffer listening to a big-mouth, jersey-wearing fan loudly proclaiming this player should skate faster, and that player should hit harder. Yet the big mouth probably can't even stand up on skates, much less skate and perform close to the level of the people he is so loudly criticizing.

Police work draws much of the same type of criticism. Critics usually appear when something goes wrong, or controversy arises. They are usually people who can't do the job themselves, and if they could, it wouldn't be near the high level of the professionals who do it successfully on a regular basis. They can also be people who will elevate their reputation or prestige at someone else's expense.

As police critics go, it seems like I would stop and throw rocks at every barking dog. As I matured and developed some wisdom and patience, I learned to try and consider the source and remind myself that most police critics probably have an agenda and couldn't do my job as well as I did it.

One night working patrol, my partner, who was a young probationary officer, and I decided to have our code-7 (lunch) at a Chinese restaurant that was located in a sketchy area downtown. It was great food, but if you went there after dark, you were living dangerously.

We parked our black and white police vehicle in front of the location in a red-zone parking curb right in front of the window where we were seated so we could see it and get to it fast if we needed to. Although a great restaurant, it had a very small parking lot for its patrons.

As my trainee and I was eating, a guy I would describe as a successful, upper-crust, arrogant yuppie-type approached us with a beautiful woman at his side. He says, "Excuse me, officers, but what gives you the right to park in a red zone when a tax-paying citizen like myself has to park only where it is legal?"

I turned to him and said, 'Well, as you can see, it's dark outside. If we took up one of the legal parking spots in the lot and you had nowhere to park, you would have to park around the corner down the dark street. In this neighborhood and at this late hour, there's a good chance that someone would have approached you, slapped you around, and who knows what he would have done with the beautiful woman you are with. Hopefully, he would only take her purse and belongings. So, to save you that embarrassment and inconvenience, I decided to park in the red."

He and his lady friend left speechless. My rookie partner could only say, "Wow."

Unfortunately, most of your critics won't be handled as "easily," and though you may hear the criticisms, have some consolation that the critic couldn't do your job. Being critical usually makes people feel good about themselves, and that's about it.

The Ultimate Roller Coaster … The Law Enforcement Career

Whenever a young person asks me questions about a law enforcement career looking for advice, I tell them that it's a great job. But I also let them know to be ready to ride the ultimate roller coaster.

For me, the roller coaster lasted 32 years, not counting the work I have done in my post-LAPD career.

Mentally, emotionally, physically, and spiritually the highs can be remarkably high, and the lows can be terribly low. Some of those lows can last for years. I experienced a "low" that lasted three years and took a real toll on me.

One of the features that attracted me to law enforcement was the fact that it's such a difficult career; not just anybody can do it successfully. I'm also including the various aspects of law enforcement, such as probation, parole, corrections, prosecutors, and not just police officers. They all have their unique challenges, and again, not just anyone can do the job. I usually advise inquiring minds that highs are high and the lows are low, and most of all, it's a marathon and not like running a 100-yard dash. The qualities that will get you to the end of your career are endurance, resilience, and enthusiasm.

Endurance is the strength and fortitude to keep pushing forward. Though I have never been a long-distance runner, running those hills in Elysian Park during the police academy helped me develop the mental endurance to push on, even when I had nothing left in the gas tank. Trust in yourself so that you can push on.

Resiliency is the ability to recover and fight back whenever things go wrong. After a few bouts with adversity, you gain the self-confidence to know you will bounce back. You're kind of like the "cockroach from hell." No matter how many times you get stepped on, once they lift their foot, you're off and running again.

Enthusiasm is the mental energy that pushes you day after day, year after year. Things like morale, working conditions, negativity, health, personal issues, and poor leadership can affect your enthusiasm; a lack of enthusiasm, endurance, and resilience leads to personal and professional suffering.

So, despite the normal challenges and obstacles life hands you, a law enforcement career will magnify them.

Knowing that, I hope you have a rewarding and mind-blowing career, and remember that the real daredevils raise their hands in the air when they are racing downhill.

That's the stuff you live to talk about.

Gang Members Care Who You Are, Not What You Are

I used to give academy recruits training on gangs. The recruits would get the gang class a week before graduation, and by then, they already knew what division they were being assigned to. I would normally get questions about specific gangs in specific divisions because a lot of the recruits wanted to know what they were stepping into, gang-wise.

During a break at one of the classes, a very attractive, blonde female recruit introduced herself, "Excuse me, Detective Moreno, I'm being assigned to Hollenbeck Division, and not being a Latino or speaking Spanish, I don't think I will be accepted there very well there."

Hollenbeck roughly covers the East Los Angeles area, and its residents are probably 90% Hispanic. I grew up in Hollenbeck Division.

This recruit had a look on her face of grave concern, but little did she know she was setting up a false barrier for herself; already thinking she didn't fit in and she wasn't even there yet. I spoke to her as if she was one of my daughters being tossed into that situation.

I explained when she leaves the academy and goes to her new assignment; she will develop a new reputation. I say "new" because one has already been developed in the academy. A new assignment usually results in a fresh start with a new reputation.

Whether it's due to work quality, ability to learn and grasp new information, handling oneself in stressful situations, and/or following instructions, you will develop a reputation with peers, superiors, training officers, citizens you encounter, and the suspects you deal with, including gang members.

You also have the added curse of being an attractive woman, so try not to let that get in the way. In a way, you might be "overly accepted." As far as your femininity is concerned, other female officers are already working there, so learn how they handle themselves in various situations, both in and out of the station. You will find some exceptional female officers who will help with any issues you might have.

As you develop your reputation, you really want to be known as fair, courteous, strong, courageous, smart, wise, and someone who takes care of business. A cop who knows her stuff.

The secret, especially with gang members, is they care who you are, not what you are. Part of being a gang member is that law enforcement is constantly sticking their nose in your business. Understanding that it is part of being a gang member, they would rather deal with specific officers. It could be because a certain officer treats them better, they think they have a certain officer snowed so they can take advantage, they may believe an officer has more influence or "juice," or they might just want to stay on a particular officer's good side to use him later on.

My point is that it has nothing to do with ethnicity, religion, gender, or race. It has to do with who you are and how you do your job. It has to do with how approachable you are, how much you are respected, and how "sharp" you are perceived to be. In other words, how much you know your stuff.

I was a Latino officer born and raised in a Latino family and immersed in Latino culture, yet I developed myself into one of law enforcement's foremost experts on Crips and Bloods black street gangs, and I'm not black.

The one true obstacle can be a language barrier, but outside of that, don't create more hurdles. It's bad enough that everyone you come into contact with, both those wearing a badge and those not wearing a badge, will be judging you. Don't create even more barriers for yourself.

It's all about how you do your job and how you treat people, simple as that.

Chapter 2
Crime and The Community

"Every society gets the kind of criminal it deserves. What is equally true is that every community gets the kind of law enforcement it insists on."
— **Robert F. Kennedy**

In Order to Help the Community, You Need to Know the Community

A black woman walked into the front desk of a police station in south/central Los Angeles and began to speak with the officer at the desk. There was no one else in the lobby at the time, so she felt comfortable openly speaking to him about what was on her mind.

The woman was a single mother living alone with her teenage daughter in an apartment building known for gang and drug activity. She was seeking some type of help, any type of help from the police.

She goes on to tell the officer that because of the gang activity at the location, the police would seem to be around a lot. Sometimes it was gang officers, and sometimes it was patrol officers, but it seemed like the police were always around.

Because the police seemed to always be around, their presence actually maintained a certain type of control over the criminals in the area. It's like everyone knew the officers were going to be around, and no one wanted to go to jail. The police presence basically kept a lid on the criminal activity and acted as a deterrent. Most of all, it made the law-abiding residents at the location feel safer.

She noticed that since the controversy started about the shooting in Ferguson, Missouri, and all of the other police shootings of black citizens, the officers haven't seemed to be around as much. Her neighbors have noticed, and for sure, the gangsters and drug dealers have really noticed. It's like they come around and hang out and are not worried about the police anymore.

The lady further stated she realized she lived in a "bad area" but was sort of desperate. She worried about her and her daughter having to be around gang members and criminals while trying to mind their own business and live their lives.

She asked the officer, "Could you and your friends begin to come by the apartment building again? Just drive by, shine your light, and look like you care. That'll make those gangsters uncomfortable, and it will help the good people out."

The woman wasn't asking for much. She was basically requesting some "extra patrol checks" where she lived. The officer obliged her and passed the word on to the other officers who worked in the area, and I'm sure that apartment building did get extra attention. Hopefully, it did some good for that lady, her daughter, and the other residents at the location,

Maybe that lady was "lucky" because, at the time she decided to go to the police station, she was able to meet with that particular officer. Or maybe that officer was "lucky" because he happened to be at the front desk when the lady walked in and gave him information to make him more effective at doing his job.

The problem is that if you want to be good and effective at what you do, you can't always depend on luck. But the harder you work, the luckier you get.

To be effective and help people, do your homework, know your job, and make your own luck happen.

I use this story about the lady and her daughter in my training, and I call it "the smell test." If some agency, politician, police chief, sheriff, administrator, or anyone else in power decides to adopt a philosophy or training that doesn't help that lady and her situation, dump it. If it does not directly or indirectly help this lady and people like her, you're not doing what's best for the people in the community and probably only catering to public opinion.

So, whenever I hear about some new, "innovative" idea regarding public safety, I check to see if it passes "the smell test" period.

If you know your community, you will know if something does and doesn't pass "the smell test."

Your Backyard Is 'Your' Backyard. Know Your Backyard Better Than Anyone Else.

I have always had great pride in my knowledge, almost to the point where I would take it personally if inquiries were being made on a particular gang or neighborhood I had been working in and I wasn't consulted first. It sounds dumb, but that's how serious I was about doing my job and knowing my stuff.

Two FBI agents who worked out of the Seattle, Washington office once visited me. They took me into an interview room, and I thought I was in trouble. They told me that they were working on a drug trafficking case and that the suspects were all gang members from a Blood set in south Los Angeles. When asking around other officers about that gang, they were told that I was "the man" in regards to knowledge of that gang. The nine gang members were arrested up in the state of Washington but claimed they either didn't know each other or were unaware that the other fellow gang members were up there as well. They were fighting the conspiracy angle of the case.

So, they threw down nine separate photos of gang members, one by one. I knew each of their nicknames, real names, and gang affiliation. One agent turned to the other and said, "Yep, he's our man."

I was flown up to Tacoma, Washington, to testify in the federal trial of those suspects. I hung around in the hallways of the court for a couple of days, waiting to testify. They kept me out of sight of the suspects who were in custody but had to march chained to each other through the hallway when going to and from the courtroom.

I noticed that when the suspects were being led in and out of the courtroom, they were loud and disrespectful, almost as if they were trying to intimidate the judge, prosecutor, jury, or anyone else within earshot. I was hiding in the hallway and could hear them acting up.

Finally, after about two days in hiding, the bailiff came out to the hallway and led me into the courtroom. I looked over at nine defendants with their nine attorneys, and all of their jaws dropped. They stared at me as if they were seeing a ghost.

I testified as to each of their names, nicknames, and gang affiliation. I also testified to how long I knew each of them and left no doubt as to my knowledge of their gang.

After my direct testimony, I was ready for the cross-examination from nine different attorneys. Oddly enough, I only got one question in total. That question was regarding one of the defendants on trial that once "aided" me in the apprehension of a rape suspect.

One of his homeboys had been wanted for rape. My partner and I saw him, and he ran into an upstairs apartment. The defendant in the trial, "Jeffrey," was hanging around with all of the other nosey people in the area, and I told him, "Hey, man. Tell your homeboy to surrender so we don't have to call SWAT and the sharpshooters out here because we aren't going anywhere." Jeffrey called out to his homeboy to surrender to us, and he did.

I testified that he did indeed help in the apprehension of a rape suspect. I don't know how much that really helped him. All of the defendants were convicted.

When I walked into the courtroom that day, those gang members were in awe of me, but in reality, they were in awe of my knowledge. Those guys were part of my backyard, and I knew my backyard. Knowing your backyard can be priceless.

If You Expect Police Work … You'd Better Condone Police Work.

A predominant perception in our 2017 society is that the public doesn't want an aggressive or proactive police force. In fact, the message to many of the "leaders" in law enforcement is that the activities and methods used by law enforcement officers must be curtailed and restrained. This becomes obvious when looking at some of the policies, training, and methods of operation adopted by certain law enforcement agencies.

The truth is certain policies, training, and methods of operation are adopted in an effort to appease a loud, disgruntled portion of the public. It turns out that in many cases, that loud disgruntled voice of the public really only represents a small segment of society. By catering to the smaller vociferous groups, we are allowing that loud voice to dictate the manner in which law enforcement conducts itself on a daily basis. That is in contrast to the original concepts of law enforcement set forth by Sir Robert Peel, considered the "original Godfather of modern-day policing" back in 1829 in London, England. In his own words, Peel stated that law enforcement must not cater to public opinion and must provide service to all members of society.

So, if a few members of the community, for whatever reason, want a softer, less aggressive approach to policing in their community, they win because they are the loudest voice. The larger silent majority segment of the community doesn't have a vote in the matter. They lose because their voice isn't heard or even considered in the matter. In this case, they don't exist.

Two things must occur to rectify this issue and ensure that law enforcement is providing service to all members of the community, not just catering to a select few.

First, when dealing with police/community relations, law enforcement leadership must do a better job of "taking the pulse" of the entire community. If you're going to do what's best for everybody, you need to know what's best for everybody. That means developing inroads so those silent voices are heard and considered when decisions are being made in regard to the welfare and safety of the entire community.

Second, if it takes a stronger, aggressive police force to make the community safe, the public must condone those methods of policing. That doesn't mean condoning police brutality or misconduct. It does mean accepting the fact that sometimes police work can be an unpleasant thing to watch. It does mean having an understanding and empathy for what the job of enforcing the law entails. It means understanding that those sworn to uphold the law and protect society from the evil that exists must be allowed to be strong and supported in their mission to do so.

The more that a law enforcement officer feels supported and allowed to do his or her job, the better job that officer will do. It's human nature.

If someone is hanging around out in front of my residence at 3:00 am with no apparent purpose, I want an officer to stop and investigate and find out what that person is up to.

If it happens to be my teenage son, we will resolve his presence being there at that time. If it is someone with no logical purpose for being there, I want that officer to establish that fact and deal with it. That is what I expect.

I condone and appreciate that the officer is doing his or her job. That makes our community safer... pretty simple.

Unfortunately, It's Easier to Give A Kid Excuses Than to Develop His Character. That Is the Lazy Person's Way of Parenting.

Parenting is the hardest job in the world, even with two involved and caring parents. Unfortunately, that's not the makeup of the "average" American family. The traditional family structure has taken a real beating over the years.

Many of the communities experiencing high crime rates, gang activity, and persistent violence contain a family unit and leadership within the home, which are overburdened and sometimes almost non-existent.

Leadership within the home is vital, regardless of whether the "leader" is a mom, dad, grandmother, grandfather, older sibling, other relative, or family friend. A child needs to learn what responsibility is, how to respect others, be a productive part of society, and how to function and grow within the rules and laws of society.

Even with a stable family unit in place, in many low-income and minority communities, a child still needs outside support to grow up and become responsible. Support people like teachers, coaches, relatives, clergy, friends, and other role models, which may include a law enforcement officer, are invaluable. Most politicians and law enforcement leaders won't tell you that for fear of being labeled a "racist."

Politicians and leaders are letting society down by playing into the excuse game, encouraging people, especially kids, young adults, and their parents, to use excuses to explain and justify bad behavior. There are no consequences for that behavior, and if there are, the excuses tend to promote leniency and avoidance of personal responsibility.

Excuses are hurting society. Many substandard parents use those excuses because it's convenient and lets them "off the hook" in regards to being responsible for their child. If the parents and family members use excuses to explain bad behavior, then that is what the child learns in order to avoid any personal responsibility.

Dr. Marin Luther King related he hoped that one day his children would be judged by society for the "content of their character and not the color of their skin. "If people nowadays were raising their children with the same concern that Dr. King had for "the" content of their character," this would be a much different world.

Don't Forget the People You'll Never Meet.

I've repeated this story many times. It's about riding with a veteran officer when I was still pretty young. We were working the graveyard shift and driving through a pretty active neighborhood at about three in the morning. On this morning, it was really quiet, and all the lights of the houses were turned off. Everyone was sleeping.

My partner, all of a sudden, pulls our police car to the curb and parks. He then says to me, "You see all of these houses with the lights off? Don't forget the people that live in them. You may never meet them, but they depend on us. That's why they can sleep at night. My point is that although people always seem to be whining about the police, not everyone feels that way. Most people respect us; we just never hear about it. Don't forget the people you'll never meet."

Thinking about the people you'll never meet can help keep you from sinking into a deep hole of negativity when you think about the public's view of law enforcement. It's easy sometimes to immerse yourself in that hole and let it affect you, your attitude, and your job.

The problem is that negativity can spill out onto the other important people and segments of your life. People may care about you, but not many want to be around negativity for very long because it can suck away the life in a room.

In high-crime neighborhoods where it can seem as though the police are not the most popular people around, the citizens might support the police, but they can't do so out in the open, especially in gang-ravaged neighborhoods. You don't even know it, but you might be the only glimmer of hope that some people have to keep them feeling safe. It happens on a regular basis, and you don't even know it.

Whenever you begin to feel that society is stacked up against the police and there's no way you can do your job and make a difference, "don't forget the people you'll never meet."

Break the Child Out of The Bubble.

I was born and raised in East Los Angeles, California. Back then, there was a very strong gang presence in the neighborhood which was made up of probably 85-90% Hispanic population. For the most part, it was a lower to middle-income area, but I was a very happy child, not focusing on what we didn't have and appreciating what we did have.

I only had one other sibling, an older sister, and my dad spent a lot of time with me. He always told me that I could be whatever I wanted to be when I grew up … as long as I could read, spell, and write. So, starting when I was 5-6 years old, he would bring home football and baseball cards, open the pack and announce the players that were in the pack. If I could spell the player's name, I could keep the card. If I couldn't spell the name, the card would go back into a pile that I could try to spell again at a later time.

It didn't take long for me to build up my card collection, but more importantly, I learned to read, write and spell. Those three qualities have helped me throughout my life and career.

My dad knew if I was to make something of myself and not be confined to living my life in a substandard lifestyle, I had to possess the qualities that would lift me out of that "stereotypical" lifestyle. I had to be able to break out of the "bubble" that our society sometimes locks kids and young people into.

If you don't have high expectations for children and then surround them with excuses for failure, you might be determining their destiny. If you expect a kid to use drugs, drop out of school, or join a gang, that's what they will probably do. If you provide them with excuses to accept the negative behavior, it makes a stronger case for them to follow that particular path.

It is up to parents, teachers, coaches, relatives, concerned citizens, and the rest of us to help break those kids out of the "pre-destined bubble" some of those kids are living in.

But that takes work, and the truth is, a lot of people are lazy or preoccupied. They would rather raise a child with excuses and allow that child to live in a "limited world," never striving to reach out and experience a life that could be.

Society doesn't allow us to criticize a person's parenting … that's too personal. So, to be politically correct, we avoid the heart of the problem and focus more on what to do when that child is in trouble. And once he or she is in trouble, we point at the "system" or the "environment" as the cause. We don't dare point at parenting.

On June 5, 2003, the Mighty Ducks of Anaheim lost Game Five of the Stanley Cup Hockey Finals 6-3 to the New Jersey Devils. I was at that game as a "guest" of Colonel Rick Fuentes, newly appointed Superintendent of the New Jersey State Police, and New Jersey Governor James McGreevy in the Governor's Luxury Suite. Watching a Stanley Cup Finals game in the luxury suite with the governor himself; is not bad for a Latino kid who was born and raised in East Los Angeles and taught how to read using football and baseball cards. I know how important it is for a kid to break out of the "bubble" because there shouldn't be a "bubble" in the first place ... but there is and maybe always will be.

Learning how to spell the names from football and baseball cards got me a seat in the Governor of New Jersey's luxury box at a Stanley Cup Finals hockey game.

How many little Latino boys born and raised in a modest home in East Los Angeles can say that?

The Greatest Myth … Everybody Hates the Police

Since I came on the job in 1975, there has been an anti-police movement. In fact, before I came on the job, there was an anti-police movement. In the Los Angeles area, on the heels of the Watts Riots in 1965, the countless anti-war (anti-authority) demonstrations, and the East LA riots, the anti-police sentiment was alive and well.

This is actually one of the things that attracted me to a law enforcement career. Being society's "unpopular underdog" and how only a special kind of person could be successful at that job. Not just anybody could do it and do it well. Challenge accepted.

Nowadays, with social media and the mainstream media being what they are, the anti-police movement appears stronger and more widespread. That's because controversial incidents like Michael Brown in Ferguson, Freddie Gray in Baltimore, Eric Garner in New York, Ezell Ford in Los Angeles, and so on are connected. In reality, one incident has nothing to do with the other, but the "movement" and the media would have you believe that all of those incidents are tied together and evidence of widespread racism among law enforcement officers across the country. The mainstream media buys into this because "sizzle" (or, in this case, controversy) sells. The world is going smoothly, and people doing nice things are not interesting news items. Instead, the media is looking for that next controversial police incident to ride the momentum of that powerful anti-police horse.

Even though I am the first to admit that police misconduct does occur, and sometimes things do go wrong, it is not to the extent that the "movement" would have you believe. In regards to law enforcement itself, things are not as bad as the perception being created as an "out of control, racist army." In reality, it's just not that way, and here are some reasons why.

First off, when a controversial incident does happen, the person involved with law enforcement is usually committing a crime or, at the very least, not complying with an officer's orders. They are out of compliance in a given situation, creating a confrontation.

Even if in each of these newsworthy, controversial incidents, the citizen involved was minding his or her own business and totally innocent of any misconduct (in most cases, it was an arrest situation), the number of those incidents is a minute fraction compared to the thousands of police/community contacts that happen on a daily basis. It's just not the widespread police brutality or misconduct that society is led to believe of today's law enforcement. If it were true, there would be thousands upon thousands of "Rodney King-type" videotapes floating around in the media and on the Internet. There aren't.

The best evidence that most people do not hate the police is that on a daily basis, police departments across the country receive hundreds of thousands of calls for service. If the police were the true enemies of the people, nobody would ever call the police. People would handle their own situations in their own way.

In many communities, supporting the police may not be popular or fashionable, but trust me: most of the people in these neighborhoods call the police, depend on the police, and want the police.

If you don't believe this to be true, visit your local agency's communications division and listen to the calls roll in. Crime statistics around the country are initiated by someone in the community reaching out to law enforcement. And we're not counting the calls for service where no report was needed or generated.

It can be challenging and difficult for law enforcement people but don't adopt the belief that everyone hates you. They don't. They may not be in a position to show their support, but they do need you and are probably amazed at how you are still able to do your job. Remember, not everyone can do what you do.

Meanwhile, those calls keep coming in.

Kids Are Always Watching You.

You may not like it. You may not have asked for it. You may not want that responsibility, but you have it.

I'm talking about being a mentor, a celebrity, or a cartoon character. That's what a police officer is because when a child looks at you, they do notice you. And when they notice you, their mind fills in the blank of what they feel about you.

The perceptions of you may originate from their parents, teachers, friends, or from what they see in the world around them. How their perceptions evolve might partially depend on you.

The classic scenario comes to mind. It's of the parent with their child, pointing at the police officer and saying, "See, if you're bad, he's going to come and take you away."

Most law enforcement officers bristle at those words and, if lucky enough, can approach the child and give a few kind words to alter the negative tone of the message. What about when you can't immediately counter those words?

There were a few times when I wasn't very proud of being a police officer. It usually involved having children around adult situations and not being able to control their perceptions of me and of the police.

When I was involved in serving search warrants or conducting probation and parole searches, on many occasions, there were children in the homes that were being searched. The routine was normally to gather the people in the residence and control them by putting them in the living room where they were "watched." This was for their safety and the safety of the personnel conducting the search.

On most occasions, the people at the residence understood what was going on and were cooperative. But even in those situations, I would notice the kids watching us with curiosity. When we would leave the residence, sometimes with an arrestee who was probably related to the child, I couldn't help but feel like "$#@."

I couldn't explain to that child that I was only there to do some "good." I couldn't explain that their brother or father may have done something bad otherwise, we wouldn't be around to bother the family.

I couldn't help that child put into context what he or she was seeing so that it minimizes the negative impact it has on that child's development into a responsible, productive human being. That is usually left up to the other people in that child's world.

If I have a regret, it's that I didn't spend more time paying attention to the kids who were watching me. I would now spend a couple of extra seconds to say hello, to ask them how they were doing, or to even just smile at them. Just a little sign to let them know I am human and I'm there for them.

One day, we served a search warrant and were leaving the residence with an arrestee and some evidence. As I was about to walk out of the house, I looked at a boy who was about nine years old standing in the living room, staring at me. I looked at him and said, "How's it going?"

A lady, who I assume was his mother, snapped at me, "Don't try to be all nice to my kid!"

I stopped and looked at her like she was crazy. The kid who was staring at me turned and also looked at her like she was crazy. He then looked back at me, and I winked. He smiled with a huge grin as I walked out the door and left.

I felt good because that kid got it and got my message.

Truancy ... The Biggest Red Flag

Years ago, I read a study that said the average reading level for an inmate entering a state prison in California for the first time was 8th grade. The study also stated that once in prison, the reading level improved. This brought me to a couple of conclusions.

First, the results of the study made sense because kids having trouble in school usually begin to lose interest in middle school grades 6 through 8. In the 8th grade, unless they are motivated and attending class, that reading level probably isn't going to rise significantly.

Once in prison and attending class and reading on their own, reading improves. That shows the inmate was capable of learning and reading at a higher level all along. He or she just wasn't interested enough at the time.

Those middle school years are critical, with multiple classes and multiple teachers for the first time. The student has the responsibility of preparing for and getting to class. They usually get more homework than they did in elementary school and have to adjust socially with the stakes a bit higher. It's an adjustment for some kids, and if there is no support in the home or anywhere else outside the classroom, they could be destined to fail.

Evidence of this "collapse" and loss of interest is truancy. It's one thing to struggle and get poor grades because a student can always get help. But failing to attend class demonstrates the student doesn't care ... or care enough.

I was on a board for the school district that would interview students with "chronic" truancy issues with their parents present. Many parents made excuses for the child, blaming the teachers, the school, the class, and the environment. But those parents weren't facing the real problem. The child was losing interest, and in most cases, they needed help to re-engage and renew their interest in attending class.

Parents would also minimize the act of their child "ditching class" by saying things like, "Well, at least he's not doing really bad things like dealing drugs and running with gangs."

Those are the kind of parents who, years later, will be saying, "Well, he only robbed the 99 cents store. It's not like he robbed a bank or something."

If you know of a kid who is ditching class and not attending school, try to get them some help or at least let the parents know. Also, let them know that truancy is a cry for help and a warning of potentially bad things ahead for that child.

That's what a red flag i

Chapter 3
Leadership

*"The most powerful leadership tool you have is your own
personal example."*
— John Wooden

People with Pride Do Better Work.

My last decade on the job, I supervised the
Department's "Gang Field Unit." Bob Ruchhoft, my
Lieutenant when I was driving around in the yellow "Pac
Man" car in the 1980s, brought me back there. He was
now the Captain of the Division.

He told me he wanted to create a squad of officers that
would work for gangs the way we did back in the 80s.
This was now 1994, and violent crime had been rampant
across the city at record levels for the past few years. He
said, "I want you guys to make a difference."

I was able to pick two officers, and that was the
beginning of the citywide "Gang Field Unit."

Over the next couple of years, we added officers and
could successfully carry out vehicular surveillance
operations. At that point, we were really good at
following people and locating and arresting wanted
criminals. Our mission was to seek out and apprehend the
most dangerous and violent gang members and career
criminals in the City of Los Angeles. The officers we were
bringing in were excellent gang officers from around the
Department. We had talent. All our talent needed was
support.

Here are a few points I focused on to make sure the
members of our squad knew they were important and
being supported –

Mission - Our direction, goals, and mission were clear.

We were to support divisional detectives by locating and apprehending suspects wanted for violent crimes committed in the City of Los Angeles. We specialized in gang members because that's where much of our expertise was.

Importance - I made our people understand that their work was important. Many of these suspects were hardcore criminals who would do anything to avoid being captured because they were looking at long prison sentences if caught. These cases were extremely difficult, dangerous, and important. Safely bringing in any of these suspects was a "big deal."

Success - I tried to make our unit successful by encouraging our members to "connect" with various detectives around the Department. So, whenever a detective solved a case and was ready for an arrest, they would contact members of our unit to get a "first crack" at the suspect before other officers and units started "beating the bushes" and potentially driving the suspect away. Divisional detectives normally didn't have the time and/or resources to track these suspects down themselves. We were successful because of the relationships we developed with the various detectives around the Department and with other agencies.

Learning - As the officer in charge of the Gang Field Unit, I encouraged their learning and development through training, meetings, conferences, and seminars. I believe the older you get and the more you learn, the better you get. The officers in our unit were also very good at teaching each other and training other law enforcement officers also.

Recognition – I tried to make sure that the unit received proper credit and recognition for their great work, and when anything came to light to our superiors involving our unit, it was something good. Any little bitches, headaches, and problems that popped up, we took care of ourselves. We kept rolling on and doing solid work. That became our reputation.

Care - The members of our squad knew they were cared for. When a couple of our officers began driving their undercover cars like "Starsky and Hutch" on our surveillance, I put my foot down. I discouraged the crazy police car driving that was normal on a TV show. When one of our officers complained that we could lose the person we were following, my reply was, "So be it." Better to lose someone we're following than to have one of our officers run a red light and take out an innocent family in a car … or kill themselves. We can always come back another day. Our people were more important than our mission … and so were our families.

I believe that these factors provided an environment where the people in our unit had great pride in their work and their effectiveness. That certainly affected how they went about doing their job on a day-to-day basis.

At one of our squad meetings, one of our officers said something that made me feel pretty good inside.

I created a three-page sheet listing a summary of the major arrests we had made during the prior 24-month period. It was pretty impressive and later got submitted for the LAPD's Meritorious Unit Award, which our unit did receive. I also wanted them to have something to share with their families, friends, and loved ones to show what they do at work.

During our squad meeting, when I passed out a copy of the document to each member of our unit, one of the guys blurted out, "Damn … I didn't know that we did this much. I just thought we were out there having a good time!"

We were …. and thank you for the compliment.

There Are No Solutions If You Don't Believe There Is A Problem

I watched the Dr. Phil Show, and it was a segment where a woman had been molested by her grandfather when she was a child.

Her story was painful enough to hear, but then they spoke with another guest on the show. It was the woman's grandmother. The grandmother allegedly didn't realize that the molestation was occurring, even though, as stated, it went on for a few years. The grandmother seemed sincerely sorry she hadn't detected a problem with her husband's behavior towards his granddaughter. However, the woman who was the actual victim of years of molestation wasn't buying her grandmother's theatrics.

The reason for the victim's hostility towards her grandmother was that on one occasion, the grandmother walked into the bedroom as the grandfather was in the act of molesting his granddaughter. The grandmother observed what was occurring and abruptly walked out of the room, almost in embarrassment.

When questioned about that allegation by Dr. Phil, the grandmother stated that she wasn't actually sure what was going on, even though both grandfather and grandchild had portions of their clothing removed.

At that point in time, that grandmother chose not to acknowledge there was a problem. She was in extreme denial, and because of that, she allowed her granddaughter to suffer years of sexual molestation. If we believe the grandmother's logic for her response and behavior, she didn't realize there was a problem, and because no problem was detected, there was no solution. No problem ... no solution.

Problems come in all shapes and sizes. Some "leaders" seem to specialize in handling the little, lightweight issues and sidestepping the big ones ... or at least look the other way as the grandmother did that day with her husband and granddaughter.

On the other hand, true leaders are there regardless of the issue, and that's why true leadership is a pleasure to watch. That's why in the law enforcement world, as in other lines of work, the majority of the "true leaders" are actually out on the frontline "truly leading." They are not primarily focused on promoting.

We were once involved in trying to arrest a gang member that was wanted for numerous murders. During the course of the confrontation with this suspect, my yellow "Pacman" police car rammed the suspect's vehicle, and the armed suspect was shot numerous times and killed.

As this was occurring, there was a veteran patrol training officer with his rookie partner who was just out of the academy handling a radio call just a block away. The training officer had 12 years on the job and was a squared-away individual I knew from working in the area.

Seconds after the shooting, the officer and his partner rolled up and asked me what had occurred. I explained the situation, and he asked what I needed. I told him, and he said he would handle it.

At that moment, that officer took control of the situation, helping to secure the scene and the crowd and "direct the oncoming" personnel on where to go and what to do. To me, it was as though the clouds in the dark night sky opened up, and a light shined down on this training officer. He became the ringmaster.

This training officer was not technically a supervisor, but he stepped up and took charge. He had the experience, knowledge, and courage to step forward and apply his talent to successfully take control of a chaotic situation.

Even as supervisors, detectives, and command staff officers arrived on the scene, this officer was providing information they needed to know and directing people to where they needed to go. Obviously, as things settled down, the "structured" chain of command settled in and took over.

But in those immediate crucial moments when the tough decisions are made, that officer stepped up and displayed true leadership and his value to his Department.

You won't see that kind of leadership hanging on a certificate from leadership school in some office in some building somewhere. It's the kind of leadership that only the people around him can see … and the type of leader that will step up and tackle a problem.

Don't be the type of person that makes rank by avoiding leadership.

Leadership Is Content … Not Image.

Years ago, while I was supervising the Citywide Gang Field Unit, we got a visit from a gang supervisor who worked for a major metropolitan police department located in the eastern United States. I won't mention his Department, and you'll soon understand why.

He jumped in with me, and we drove down to Southeast Station in Watts because that's where our unit's operation was going to happen. We were going to be looking for a gang member that had committed several-armed robberies.

The supervisor was a real nice guy and enjoyed touring around Los Angeles, especially some of the gang areas. We got to Southeast Station about 3:30 pm in time to see the change of watch in the parking lot where the officers working Day Watch were coming to the station to be relieved by the officers that were working PM Watch. So there were a lot of uniform patrol officers going to and from the station.

The supervisor was very impressed with the appearance of the officers. Everybody, for the most part, looked neat and clean, with no goatees, long hair, or ponytails on the male officers, like with this supervisor's Department. For the most part, the officers looked very sharp and in shape on this "average" LAPD patrol day.

We completed our unit briefing in the parking lot, away from the rest of the officers and foot traffic. We discussed assignments, the suspect, the location, and what we expected to happen if we were to be successful on this day.

When the supervisor and I got back into my car, his jaw dropped. I came to find out where he worked, and a supervisor would not be involved in the takedown and arrest. He and the other supervisors would stay away until either the suspect was arrested or the operation came to an end for whatever reason.

He looked at me like I was either crazy or stupid and wanted to know the reasoning of having a supervisor present during a field operation.

I explained to him that as their supervisor, one of my responsibilities (among a few others) was to ensure that the team could be successful in their endeavors. Since I had a lot of experience and was the person in charge, I thought of myself as more of a player/coach. The mission we were charged with was difficult, and each operation had its own unique set of circumstances.

As a "player/coach," I was more of an overseer, and with most of these dangerous suspects, the more experienced minds, the better. By no means were these operations a one-man show, and every team member had input; decisions were made at very crucial times. I couldn't see myself sitting in the office while something bad might occur.

Plus, as an on-scene supervisor, I could clear the way for our people to do their work and not deal with obstacles as they popped up, such as concerned citizens, other officers, other agencies, and command staff, especially when something did go down, such as an arrest. Most of our suspects were located in divisions and jurisdictions other than where they originally committed the crime they were wanted for. In some incidents, a supervisor was necessary to smooth over any number of issues. That should be the job of the person in charge, and that is part of a leader taking care of his or her people.

These were things that probably had never crossed the supervisor's mind before. Or maybe things he had never concerned himself with. Luckily for me, I was taught by the best and had the opportunity to see the best in action as it pertains to frontline leadership.

I would much rather take part in the grind and be involved in the actual process than have my picture taken at the podium after the fact at a press conference. With leadership, there is "frosting," and there is "cake." The frosting is sort of the image of the cake; some cakes look way better than they taste.

In leadership, the important part is the cake, not the frosting. The frosting just looks good.

There Is No "I" In Team, But There Is An "I" In Win. Have Enough of An Ego to Be A Strong Team Member … And Leader.

Going through life, many times I have heard the cliché', "There is no 'I' in team." That may be true, but there is an 'I' in "win." What I mean is that to be a good team member, you have to be strong enough to carry your share of the load and even be ready to step in and lead if need be.

As a training officer, my style was as I was teaching. I spoon-fed confidence into my probationer. My logic was as long as the rookie was learning and picking up the key fundamentals of the job, he or she deserved to develop enough mental strength to make a crucial decision if my back happened to be turned.

I've seen training officers who were extremely tough on their rookies, and that's fine if the process turns out a quality cop. But I've also seen rookies who were so afraid of making a mistake that when the time came, they'd freeze up and make no decision at all. Most of the time, in law enforcement, that is not a good thing.

If I am occupied, and someone is walking up behind me, I want my probationer to have the nerve and confidence to step up and intercept that person, protecting me. Once finished with the probationary period, that officer should be confident and settled enough to work on his or her own if need be. As that officer's career progresses, so should their knowledge, experience, and confidence. To me, that is creating a solid or "strong" officer; and a strong employee is a strong team member, and that applies to most lines of work, not just law enforcement.

I coached youth soccer for many years and still enjoy watching my grandkids play various sports. Some coaches are so vocal and overbearing that the kids playing for them are not allowed to think or make decisions. A good example is when the coach is talking to the child who is at bat after every pitch. The kid is not allowed to figure out how to deal with that pitcher they are up against and must also worry about what the coach is saying to him or her. I understand coaching and guidance, but to some degree, they need to experience things for themselves as well.

Many of the best youth coaches I have seen keep their dialogue to a minimum. Practice is the time to prepare ... the game is the time to execute ... ideally. As you help that young player prepare for game situations, you are making them a stronger person. A team full of strong, confident individuals is the basis for a strong team.

When someone talks about there being "no I in team," they are referring to someone who is selfish and can't keep their ego in check, thus disrupting the team concept. You can be strong, confident, knowledgeable, and with an ego and still know your place in a team setting. In fact, those qualities make you a more desirable team member.

You may have to learn how to check your ego to play nicely with others and not always be the center of attention, but I've never met a solid player who didn't have a solid ego.

I guess you could say the same for cops, too.

A Bad Solution Just Creates More Problems.

If you have a hole in the roof and your house is getting flooded, installing more aluminum gutters along the sides of your house is not going to solve the problem. The inside of your home is still getting flooded regardless of the number of gutters you install.

Have enough "courage" or sense to admit you're going to have to fix that hole or pay a professional to do it. Even though it may be expensive, face the problem, assess it, and repair it before the situation gets worse. This is what is happening with the criminal justice system.

Although violent crime is up across the country, law enforcement leadership held a meeting in October 2016 with 130 police chiefs to address the number of ways to "reduce the prison population." They were figuring out how to put up better gutters on the house while the hole in the roof was getting bigger.

Leadership doesn't have the courage to go into some of these communities and say, "We're having a problem with the way some children are being influenced and led into a life of crime, gang activity, and drug abuse. We want to teach kids how to avoid the criminal justice system and be productive, responsible individuals."

To release people from prison and/or decriminalize certain crimes doesn't help those kids with the negative influences around them. We should want them to avoid trouble at all costs and not provide excuses when they do get in trouble. The message here is that if you screw up, you'll get a second chance, a third chance, and maybe even a fourth. That is not the message I want to be sent to my child.

True leadership isn't easy, safe, or convenient. But true leadership means doing the right thing regardless of how uncomfortable that might be.

That is unselfish, courageous, and leadership.

Respect Comes in All Sizes.

I remember a story about Peyton Manning while he was playing for the Denver Broncos and his return to Indianapolis to play a football game against the Colts.

The camera followed him around when he got to the stadium. It showed his interactions with members of the Colts' staff and the stadium personnel. He was greeted with handshakes, hugs, and other nice gestures from the people there.

Someone mentioned to the camera that people just loved him. When asked why, the reply was because "he was nice to everyone and treated everybody with respect. From the owner of the team to the janitors in the building, he was good to everyone."

That was a leadership lesson and gave me a different impression of Peyton Manning as a person. I saw his leadership in that film clip. Years later, Peyton would hobble into the Super Bowl and lead his Denver Broncos to an NFL Championship over a highly-favored Carolina Panthers team. Most experts believed that Denver was overmatched by a skyrocketing Carolina team and didn't have much of a chance to win. Manning probably wasn't 100% physically and statistically had not played up to his level. But Manning didn't "duck the fight" and chose to play despite the odds against him and his team.

Manning played the entire game, and despite the odds against him and his team, the Denver Broncos won Super Bowl 50 over Carolina, 24-10. He did what leaders do, the right thing in the face of the negative odds. He also does something else that leaders do. He treats everyone with respect and uses the same voice and demeanor with all.

Watching a janitor give Peyton Manning a hug when he saw him showed me that leadership comes in all sizes. If you are in a leadership position and caught up in your rank and stature, you might want to see that Peyton Manning film clip. It would be good for you. It reminds us that rank is what you are, not who you are. Don't get caught up in it.

If You Lose the Frontline, You've Lost the Game.

There is a major morale problem in law enforcement across the United States. The job is a challenging one, and there always seems to be controversy. However, this time, it is a nationwide conflict that pits law enforcement management against frontline workers. It doesn't seem to matter what the exact assignment or job is; the problem is affecting people working in probation, parole, corrections, and prosecution, as well as police officers and sheriff deputies.

The sad thing is that many law enforcement leaders rush to academic philosophy for methods, training, and solutions to many of the policing problems society faces. Employing a method based on research that is deemed as successful or "best practices" relieves that leader from using his own initiative and courage to deal with issues in his own city. If the process fails or is unsuccessful, he was just using a "proven" practice currently being used by executives, professionals, and leaders across the nation.

Frontline officers everywhere are aware of the infatuation their leaders have with those credentialed experts, and it creates resentment and dissension among the ranks. Those frontline people with their valuable, hands-on experience should be involved in the problem-solving process, but most of the time, their opinion and input are not considered in the equation and are referred to as simply "anecdotal." The academics and consultants equate anecdotal with being unreliable, unscientific, and/or not based on data-driven research.

After ignoring the very people doing the work and bringing in research-based training, one expects these knowledgeable people to embrace the "new and improved" method and discard anything they've ever learned. They discard what made them successful in the first place and employ what could be termed as excessive hierarchal thoughts, ideas, and solutions flowing from the top down, not in both directions, as they should be.

Add to this resentment that management appears to be responding to public opinion and not acting on behalf of everyone, including their employees. Leadership seems to be jumping through hoops to make the negative noises stop. The more they jump, the louder the noise gets. That's why making a lot of noise works. It's called intimidation, and it's making law enforcement rethink much of its training, policies, and procedures.

If management wants things to work better with the frontline, my advice is to have some faith in your people and include them in the problem-solving process. Don't have a knee-jerk reaction when a controversial situation occurs. If you feel so compelled to rely on academic experts, combine their knowledge with something they don't have, firsthand experience. Have them work with the best frontline people to develop strategies and solutions.

I'm not against academics and scholars in law enforcement; I'm against how they are used. They are perceived to be more valuable than the experienced professionals who actually do the job.

To be effective at working gangs, you must understand the concept of "respect." You realize that "respect" is a two-way street. I'm surprised that the concept of respect isn't taught in most leadership and supervisory courses. It should be taught because today's law enforcement leadership is surely missing an opportunity with their frontline people.

My last message to the law enforcement leaders out there…

If you lose the frontline, you've lost. So, start earning

your money and sincerely care about what you're doing. If not, get out of the way and let someone else do the job.

Unfortunately, the problem is that most leaders can be ineffective and still pick up a regular paycheck.

Now, that is a "participation trophy."

Cop World Versus the Real World

Most law enforcement people are good, decent, well-meaning individuals who all want the same things in life. We all want the "American Dream." Good job, good wages, raising a family in a safe neighborhood, and a better world overall. After all, part of the reason we do what we do is to make the world a better place. We tend to be idealistic in that way.

The problem is that as "cops" (law enforcement), we sometimes believe if we do something with no malice or bad intentions and it doesn't hurt anyone or isn't against the law; it should be fine. That isn't always true. Sometimes our actions are judged in the "real world, not the "cop world," and that can be a problem.

The value of having experience, especially as a supervisor, is it allows us to see things up ahead the "mere mortal" team member may not be able to see. In my training for law enforcement officers, I show a picture of a calm swimming pond in a nature setting. The average person wants to go swimming in the pond, but the experienced supervisor stops them. The average person sees the calm surface of the pond, while the experienced supervisor knows what is lurking below the surface and prevents anyone from jumping into the unsafe water.

In that scenario, the "cop world" is the seemingly harmless act of jumping into the inviting swimming pool. The supervisor was strong enough to prevent it because there would have been harm done to whoever jumped in the water. Nowadays, a harmless act of jumping into the pond could be like posting something funny but borderline offensive on social media. You might think, "What's the big deal?" If it's something that can affect your job or make your life harder, what's the point?

Even though I may have been supervising responsible, grown-up adult people, I sometimes felt as though I was the parent in the group. That's not necessarily a bad thing, as you are expected to keep people safe and out of trouble the best way you can.

There are quite a few instances when the leader or supervisor felt it was more important to be accepted by the group than to keep them out of trouble. When that happens, someone gets hurt or in trouble.

It takes special courage to risk not being popular with the people being supervised, but if you are acting on their behalf and for the welfare of the unit, that is what you're supposed to do. That is, you are being strong enough to be a leader. That is your experience, judgment, and wisdom taking charge to save one or more from some unforeseen grief up ahead. It's when one of your subordinates says to you, "I didn't agree with you at the time, but now I see why you did what you did ... thanks."

And if you can't stop your child from touching a hot stove, maybe you shouldn't be a parent ...

'Equanimity' ... My Leadership Style

Equanimity means having mental or emotional stability or composure, especially under tension or strain.

Another way of describing equanimity is that it's a state of psychological stability and composure that is undisturbed by experience of or exposure to emotions, pain, or other phenomena that may cause others to lose the balance of their mind.

To me, it means while everything around you is going up in flames, you are able to keep your head (senses), focus and continue to move forward, making progress in completing the task and/or achieving the goal.

I recall an example of "equanimity" that occurred

during the 1992 Rodney King Riots in Los Angeles.

I was assigned as a CRASH Detective Supervisor at Northeast Detectives in the Highland Park area of Los Angeles. Working 12-hour shifts due to civil disobedience occurring in south Los Angeles and to a portion of the city just west of downtown in the Rampart Area,

I had a squad of 10 detectives, and our job was to wait at the station and respond as a squad to any location requested to assist in keeping order. After all, there was a riot going on.

I met with my squad and told them when we hit the field, we were going to focus on our specific task, complete it and return back to the station to await additional assignments. We would stay together as a unit in our four black and white police vehicles and not wander or get distracted away from our squad and our particular mission. We would all be on the same page.

I stayed field oriented in my work, so I had no problem working outside and being tactically proficient. Working with CRASH Detectives, we arrested some of our suspects, so I stayed up on my tactics. I was comfortable in the field. Some people in the other detective squad weren't, so I was wondering what was going to happen if they had to go into the field on a mission.

There was another squad of detectives at the station on the same watch that received a separate mission. Our assignment was to proceed to the Ralph's Market located at 3rd Street and Vermont Ave in Rampart Division and clear out the store. With the riots in full throttle, looters had overrun the store, and their security needed help in "reclaiming" the market.

We gathered up in our four police cars and caravanned to our assignment, entered the store, and cleared it of looters. Most of the looters did not respect store security officers but had respect for the LAPD uniforms, so they left in fear of being arrested.

It was a weird atmosphere driving toward the Ralph's

Market on Vermont Ave because it was daylight, people were in the streets, but there wasn't a lot of traffic. In most places, nobody was obeying the traffic laws because you didn't want to get stuck at a red light with a hostile, unpredictable crowd around you.

The police radio was also crackling hard with calls of "415 groups", "arson suspects," and "shots fired" coming from various parts of the riot-affected city. It was surreal, for sure.

I told my squad we would return to Northeast Station the same way we drove to Ralph's. We would stay together and not get distracted unless faced with a life-or-death situation. If that were to happen, we would stay together as a squad.

So, we trailed back to Northeast Station all in one piece as a squad. We had been gone about an hour and a half when I checked back in with my lieutenant. He was happy that we made it back safely but was upset because the other squad did not return from their mission also in Rampart Division.

He lost contact with them, didn't know their status, and was really concerned when four of their detectives returned to the station without the rest of the squad. And they didn't know where the rest of the squad was. They eventually showed up at the station, but I wouldn't have wanted to be the supervisor in charge of that squad when they got back.

This was a good lesson in "equanimity" because although the city was literally burning to the ground, by keeping our composure, focusing on our strategy, and carrying out our plan, we were successful. Watching the other squad fall apart in their mission reinforced the value of "equanimity." Of course, having experience, confidence, and focus really helped.

Equanimity, a very cool word.

Chapter 4
Officer Safety

It's how you show up at the showdown that counts."
— **Homer Smith**

Who Is More Dedicated ... You or Your Opponent

When training law enforcement officers, I bring up this topic accompanied by a photo of a gang member I took at Tamara Prison in Tegucigalpa, Honduras. The gang member's face is covered with tattoos, most of them gang tattoos giving him a very sinister and intimidating look.

I follow up with the comment, "I notice that none of you have your agency or unit tattooed on your face. Does that mean that this gang member is more dedicated than you?"

That answer should be "no," but looking at that gang member with tattoos can make one wonder who is more dedicated, him or you? To me, dedication is a mental state that measures commitment to a task or cause, like a job or mission.

To analyze my level of dedication, you'd have to cut me open and take parts of my heart, brain, and soul to get an accurate reading. You can't measure my dedication by reading my forehead. To me, that's just a prop or tool to help gain a psychological advantage over another person. With gang members and the general public, it works.

I have learned over the years to focus on the task at hand of gaining control of a situation by using sound tactics and methods. When everyone is under control and things are safe, I may then check out any unique or noteworthy characteristics, such as tattoos.

I don't let people have a psychological edge over me by

using their props. That's a decision and mindset developed ahead of time, so when pulling a car over and a scary monster exits, you're not covering your eyes and cowering like a frightened child.

When the scary monster gets out of his car, and he sees that I'm not distracted by his "look" and I'm taking care of business, he will know that I am as dedicated to my cause as he is to his, probably more so. No punks here.

Two Things I Know Can Erase Fear … "Anger" And "Focus."

It's been my experience that the mind has two ways to overcome fear. This is very important for officer safety because encountering situations that can produce fear is part of the job. Those two qualities that act as erasers are "anger" and "focus."

Anger can overcome fear, but anger is an emotional response that can make a person "undisciplined." At that point, it can alter judgment and cause personal harm. There were numerous instances when an officer used anger to overcome a situation. The problem is that an officer's anger can get him in trouble. So even though you may have met a dangerous challenge with anger and prevailed, the anger can cause a bigger issue than the original problem, to begin with. That is why a solid partner or supervisor can help keep an angry officer out of trouble.

Focus can also overcome fear, but it is "disciplined" and can be a guide through dangerous and critical situations.

Focus is relying on experience, training, proficiency, and mental sharpness to be at your best. The goal or object of your actions is to use your talent to complete your mission,

You focus on the task at hand, whether it is a carload of gang members being pulled over, a combative inmate being extracted from a cell, or the front door on a narcotic search warrant being breached.

Focus brings all of those positive qualities together. The more prepared, the sharper the focus will be. The sharper the focus, the better you will handle the stress, pressure, and challenge of the situation. That's what a professional, seasoned officer does.

Anger is an emotion that needs to be controlled and kept in check. Focus is the method by which you operate and do the job and should only improve with time.

There will be moments when you'll look back on a certain situation and ask yourself, "Wow, how in the world did I do that?"

It was the focus, my friend.

The More You Know, The Safer You Are

If you were going to use an ATM at night to withdraw some cash and you knew at this particular ATM, two guys were going to rob you and shoot you; you'd probably use a different ATM.

If you knew that on a Sunday morning, while driving to church and passing through a certain intersection, an elderly lady in her vehicle was going to run a red light and smash your car, you'd probably take a different route.

Those are two examples of information if you had would make you much safer. It may not really matter how that information finds you because there are countless ways to gain and receive information. But now that you have the information, you can use it.

Information is the raw data received and refined to solve a case, answer a question on a test, or determine if a person is right for you. Information is processed through your brain to determine how useful it is. The more information used and developed, the more experience and success acquired. This should be an ongoing process and will continue throughout your personal and professional life.

Based on this philosophy, too much information is better than not enough. I can have tons of information, but if I can sort through and figure out that the elderly lady is going to run that red light, that tiny bit of information may have saved my life.

On the other hand, if I never receive the information about the elderly lady in her car, it won't help me, and I am at the mercy of my fate. Law enforcement can do everything right, and things can still go wrong. With training, experience, and knowledge, the best we can do is put the odds a little more in our favor.

How you deal with coworkers, superiors, subordinates, suspects, or the public, your attitude, and your personality will have a significant effect on whether you are receiving information or not. If people don't like you or are uncomfortable being around you, overall effectiveness is weakened.

I have been around officers who sincerely didn't care what their coworkers or members of the public thought of them. That's fine, and good macho talk while you're hanging out with your boys, but are you cheating yourself? Are people with vital bits of information simply bypassing you?

There are thousands of ways to gain information, some work for some people and not for others. Figure out what works and when it works for you. Ideally, you want to become an "information magnet."

Understand that in being an information magnet, information must run in two directions. It can't be "Give it to me, and I give you nothing." You won't stay in business very long, or at least not effectively.

In the process of becoming an information magnet, you begin to learn who the other "magnets" are and work to develop a solid relationship with those people. That is how to develop your "network."

It sounds easy, but it's not, and it takes time … and effort. But it is worth it.

Information is important because it could save your life or the life of someone you care deeply about. Think about that as you're doing your job. The more you know, the better off and safer you are …

The Most Important Vehicle Stop in The History of Law Enforcement … Could Be Your Next One.

I was training at a law enforcement conference in Atlantic City, New Jersey. When I was done with class, an officer who had worked the graveyard shift approached me. He said he came straight over to the training because he didn't want to miss the class.

We had a nice conversation, and I was humbled he stayed up after working all night. The officer asked me a couple of questions and seemed to be very modest about working for a small police agency. He was impressed because I worked at LAPD and remarked he sometimes wondered what it would be like to work for a famous agency like that. I stopped him in his tracks and told him two things.

First off, the biggest and baddest criminal in his small town was probably just as big and as bad as anyone in LA. Some places just have more of them.

Secondly, even though he may work for an agency that most people never heard of, any car he pulls over is just as important as any car being pulled over in LA, Chicago, or New York. Just because they work in a larger agency doesn't mean what they are doing is more important, and certainly doesn't mean those officers are more important. We are all important.

It is dangerous to become complacent in police work. It is just as dangerous to minimize or underestimate the inherent perils in the work environment. It is hazardous to believe, "That kind of violence isn't going to happen here. This is not Chicago or Los Angeles." It could happen "here" and land right in your lap when it does.

Be prepared. If you are "over-prepared" for the next 25

years and "the big one" never happens, all the better. At least you were ready and willing in case it did.

The next car being pulled over, the next cell extraction or the next probation search can all be very important. If something goes wrong, there won't be the next promotion, the next Super Bowl, or the next child's birthday party to get the house ready for. You won't be going home to your family or anywhere else for that matter.

It doesn't matter who you are or where you work. That next car you pull over might be the most important vehicle stop in the history of law enforcement.

Or at least the most important in your history.

Just Because You Think Someone Is A Punk Doesn't Make Them A Punk

In 1988 and 1989, I addressed the University of Southern California Trojan football teams, giving the players insight into how life was in south/central Los Angeles especially concerning the gang problem.

Larry Smith was the football coach, and I had a couple of good talks with him. He wanted the players to be aware of the issues involved in wandering off campus to socialize. Many of his players were not from Southern California and did not know the areas of the city to stay away from.

The first time I addressed the team was memorable for me because Junior Seau was getting a good ribbing from some of the players for something he had done at practice. He took it well, and it seemed he was a great guy that was good for the team and in the locker room. I would realize years later that this happened to be the Hall of Famer Junior Seau.

A key message I shared was that looks can be deceiving. I described a scenario in which a couple of them are out late, grabbing some food at the local Fatburger, where everyone goes for some late-night grub. You're standing in line and accidentally bump into some teenage kid half your size. The kid is upset about the bump and wants to make a big deal about it. On the inside, you're laughing because you know you can squash this "punk" like a grape. Despite the obvious size and strength advantage and the fact there are three of you, this kid is still not backing down. Why is that?

I go on, "he is not backing down because, based on his hostile, trouble-making attitude, he is probably a gang member who is carrying the 'equalizer' in his waistband. He wouldn't think twice about capping your ass, especially to avoid getting his butt whipped."

I ended this particular lesson with some advice, "Just because you think someone is a punk doesn't make them a punk."

As I use the term "punk" in training and in connection with this part of the book, I refer to the Merriam-Webster Dictionary definition of "a usually petty gangster, hoodlum, or ruffian." To me, this is someone trying to be rough, tough, and significant but who really isn't. In this context, it is demeaning, so you are really putting the individual down by thinking or referring to them as a punk.

When working in law enforcement, it can be very easy to elevate yourself in your mind regarding your proficiency, tactics, and decision-making skills and assume everything will turn out fine because it usually does. We know this is not always true, and things happen.

To operate at a top level, keep mentally, physically, and emotionally prepared for all challenges. But even with all of your preparation, you will cheat the odds of coming out on top if you underestimate your opponent. Like the big, hulking USC football player standing in line at Fatburger staring at an irritated teenager half his size thinking, 'This guy is a punk,' you are placing yourself at risk.

Many years ago, I was speaking at a gang symposium in

Chiapas, Mexico, and I had the pleasure of meeting a priest who was operating a "safe house" in Honduras for gang members that wished to leave gang life. The safe house existed because many of those gang members were tattooed all over their faces, which made them a target for fellow gang members who were upset they left the gang, the rival gang members who were still rivals, law enforcement personnel hunting down gang members and vigilantes who believed in taking the law into their own hands. Those gang members and their families had to hide somewhere.

The priest facilitated the safe house for many years and came into contact with hundreds of gang members and their family members. He interviewed most of them, and based on those interviews, he told me a horrendous statistic. He estimated at least 70% of the gang members he dealt with had been sexually molested and/or abused as children. He believed the number was higher, but some of the gang members interviewed were too ashamed to admit being victimized.

He explained that these gang members came to him as "very broken individuals, and he meant broken on many levels. He then gave me a bit of advice to pass on to my American friends in law enforcement. He has met some of the most dangerous people in the world, and they are those who have no hope and nothing to lose. In his words, the most dangerous person is one with nothing to lose."

And if you don't know the individual, you don't know what he is capable of. As an officer, you might be standing over someone half your age lecturing him and have no idea who you're talking to. That kid might be one of those broken people with no conscience or sense of guilt. That kid could be deadly to you if the opportunity ever presented itself.

This is the reason why those professionals that have worked in gangs for some time dislike the term "wanna-be." When you call someone a "wanna-be," you might tend to underestimate him. At what point is that 14-year-old possible gang member no longer a wanna-be? When he runs from you and fires a shot at you, narrowly missing your head? Is he still a wanna-be?

When doing your job, be attentive, vigilant, and sharp. But don't make the mistake of assuming that someone is punk because they might surprise you, and tactically speaking, we don't like surprises.

When a suspect looks into your eyes to see what's inside, you better hope he sees a 'warrior.'

A controversial issue for law enforcement is the "warrior versus guardian" concept. There are those who believe that an officer's "warrior mindset" gets him into trouble and creates real problems in the officer's dealings with the public.

They believe that starting in the police academy, officers are taught survival techniques, and a part of that is developing a warrior mindset. They believe that mindset is harmful in dealing with the public and that today's officer lacks "emotional intellect." So, they push a philosophy of de-escalation and make the officer's safety a secondary concern.

For a police executive to tell a group of officers to "dump the warrior mentality" and adopt a "guardian mindset" is demeaning and lacks insight. During a normal shift, a patrol officer will wear many hats depending on the situation. That officer may be a counselor, teacher, parent, adviser, referee, babysitter, mediator, and/or coach. "Warrior" and "guardian" are just two more of the many roles the frontline officer must fulfill.

The bottom line is these academics and executives aren't going to be with you when entering a residence to deal with a family dispute and a house full of angry people. They will be home sitting by the fireplace and sipping on a choice glass of wine. If you don't make it out of that house alive, it must have been something YOU did wrong. It certainly wasn't due to their enlightened philosophy and training.

I don't believe an officer's safety should be placed in jeopardy due to some academic insight, especially when the philosophy comes from people who have never done the job ... or at least not as extensively as many frontline officers have.

Law enforcement managers, academic experts, and politicians can examine, critique, and control their officers as much as they want. The problem with enlightened training is the minds designing it can't account for the actions of the people officers deal with. They are too busy telling an officer how to think, when to think, and what to think. It's creating "paralysis by analysis."

Time after time, there are examples of how an officer's warrior mentality has helped them through perilous situations and kept him or her alive. You use discretion, experience, and logic to figure out how to handle the situation you know nothing about until you are experiencing it. That's why you must have that warrior spirit inside you and be ready for when you need it.

There will come a time when a suspect will decide whether to cooperate or take you on. That decision can be determined by what that suspect sees in your eyes. Let's hope that the suspect sees a 'warrior.'

De-Escalation Is A Decision Made by An Officer in A Particular Situation. It's Not the Mindset That You Carry Around with You.

A popular philosophy being advocated by many academics, experts, and law enforcement leaders is that of "de-escalation."

De-escalation is nothing new. What is new is the idea that an officer must be in a "de-escalation mindset," especially when approaching a situation before the variables are known. Academics and members of management insist they want officers to act as "guardians of democracy" who serve and protect instead of warriors who conquer and control it.

De-escalation is a tool and technique that an officer uses when that officer feels it is appropriate. It is one of many tools an officer may use, but it is not a mindset.

To quote one of the "experts" in the use of force controversy, "You may have a conflict where it is necessary for an officer to puff up and quickly take control. But in most situations, it's better if officers know how to de-escalate, calm things down, slow down the action."

This individual minimizes the act of "taking control," which is a key element in officer safety. They also say, "in most situations," it's better if officers know how to de-escalate. No kidding, it's part of logic, critical thinking, and common sense. This was taught as part of the use of force scale in training, knowing when to apply the appropriate amount of force.

They are sacrificing officer safety to promote a philosophy that certain people will benefit from both financially and in stature. This is why so many frontline officers are rejecting the philosophy and losing faith in management. They are using a repackaged old tool and placing a name on it to appeal to the current environment embroiling law enforcement.

The well-known Chinese General and war-strategist Sun Tzu said over 2,500 years ago, "The supreme art of war is to subdue the enemy without fighting." So apparently, this new concept of de-escalation has actually been around for a few thousand years.

In 1975 when I was in the academy, it was called "talking your suspect to jail," and it still is. This is not a new concept in police work. Certain academic types are just trying to convince society that police officers throughout history never knew of this concept and basically chose to brutalize people.

In reality, be whoever you need to be to safely get the job done. Your mindset is your mindset, and your emotions, intelligence, and common sense are but some of your tools. Use them to aid you, not confuse you.

Unfortunately, an officer recently responded to a radio call at a restaurant regarding a transient who was causing a disturbance. In an attempt to defuse the situation, the officer slid into a booth with the suspect and asked him how he was doing.

The suspect responded by pulling out a handgun and shooting the officer point blank in the head, killing him.

The "de-escalation" crowd was not around to comment.

De-escalation is a tool in your toolbox and a strategy, not a mindset. Use it when your experience and instincts tell you it's appropriate. If a 'warrior mindset' is what makes you successful in your service to the community, then that's what you are.

What Kept Me Alive? ... My Situational Awareness

Situational awareness is keeping track of where, who, and what is around you and what is happening in your immediate environment. It is your current surroundings and being aware of your own capabilities so that you can react to sudden changes in those surroundings. The people that know this better than anyone are those of you who work in correctional facilities.

Back in 1985, I worked with the Los Angeles County Sheriff's Operation Safe Streets (OSS) gang unit in the LA County Jail. They gave me a desk in their office, and I wore my navy blue LAPD raid jacket while I was working in the jail. We can say that I stood out because, at that time, I was the only person working in the entire jail and wearing a blue LAPD raid jacket.

After the first week of wearing that jacket, the Crip and Blood modules got used to it, and it wasn't a big deal in the jail amongst the inmates. As you can imagine, the LAPD didn't have many fans in the LA County Jail. My head was always on a swivel, checking out who was around me and what they were doing. On some days, even when it was uneventful, I'd go home pretty drained because it took a lot of energy to constantly engage inmates and keep track of my surroundings. My safety depended on situational awareness.

I've talked to quite a few officers who have been shot and/or involved in deadly confrontations with suspects. I have also experienced a few myself, and the consensus that carried many of them successfully through the situation was thinking about that type of situation beforehand. Thinking about those types of situations and being mentally prepared.

I coached Little League baseball for a few years, and one of the best drills was creating situations with base runners and setting up the players on the field. I might have runners on first base and third base, and one out. Then I would ask various players on the field, "If the ball is hit to you, what would you do?"

The next situation might be a runner on third base and nobody out. What would you do? Because each player could analyze the situation before the ball was hit to them, they could make their decision with less anxiety and confusion. It also gave them the confidence to know that they were ready to make the play. It was an effective way of working on their "situational awareness."

The best advice I can give is to constantly work on situational awareness. As you gain experience and add that experience to common sense, alertness, tactical proficiency, and knowledge, you will become more prepared.

Recognizing a situation as it plays out and being aware of one's own capabilities will assist in making the best tactical decisions and staying alive. I have gone through a million situations in my head, even after I retired, and it is never a waste of time.

As well-known author and Crip gang member "Monster Kody," Scott once told me, "There are two kinds of cops. There's the one that if you punch him in the face and he sees his own blood, his brain will melt down, and he'll freeze up. Then there's the other kind that when he sees his own blood, he gets mad, and the fight is on."

The second kind of officer knows that just because he may be bleeding, he is not defeated, and the fight is not over.

Be the "fight is still on" kind of person...

Chapter 5
You

"If I knew I was going to live this long, I'd have taken better care of myself."
— Mickey Mantle

You Can't Change People, But You Can Make Them Think

When I'm conducting training or speaking to law enforcement officers, my goal is to make them think. When talking to a crowd of 200 to 300 people, there is a wide spectrum of experience, knowledge, and expertise. There will also be a variety of attitudes, especially with law enforcement officers.

Cops are a tough crowd. They are tough because they are in a unique career that can have life-or-death implications with each decision. Plus, cops are very competitive. If they weren't, they wouldn't be sitting in your class, to begin with. They competed and beat out a lot of other people for that job. Sometimes when making a suggestion or giving advice, you almost become the enemy if the perception is that you are arrogantly talking down to the crowd with "your" special knowledge. Trust me, I have sat in a crowd and listened to a good speaker gets torn apart by people talking negatively under their breath.

When I conduct training, ideally, my goal is to pass on information an officer can use either on the job or in their life. It would be great to pass on meaningful thoughts and words, but realistically, I'll settle for making them think.

I want those who I am engaging with to rethink their

thought processes, their attitudes, their tactics, and their decision-making skills. It's not that what I am saying is right or wrong, but if it makes you analyze how you do your job, I'm winning as an instructor.

If I am challenging you mentally, emotionally, and to some extent, spiritually, I am doing my job. I have awakened your thought process and created some energy where complacency may have set in.

So, whether the class is one hour or eight hours, if I can make you think, then we both win.

I've been conducting training for law enforcement officers since 1982, and the best compliment I still receive is, "Thanks for the training. I do a lot of what you talked about. I've just never heard it put in words before. Thank you."

If you're good at what you do, you're going to make enemies. To shut them up, keep being good at what you do.

In law enforcement, if you are good at what you do, you are going to make enemies. I'm not talking about the criminals or people on the other side of the law. I'm talking about people on "your side of the fence." They can be co-workers, colleagues, and members of a peer group and not necessarily someone in a superior or subordinate relationship. It is usually someone that makes you ask yourself, 'What's his or her problem? I have no issue with them.'

This is a competitive field, and whatever success you may have is overshadowing someone else's performance, or that's the perception they have. I had a situation where I wasn't trying to show anybody up or make anyone look bad. I was just doing my job as I normally did. In this particular scenario, other members of this unit were cruising along at 20 miles per hour, and I was going more like 30 mph. They didn't see it as my success, making the entire unit look good. They felt I was making them look bad, which was not my intention. Luckily in this situation,

I had a good supervisor who was very supportive, and that really helped me. He knew I loved my job and was doing good work, and as my boss, he had no complaints.

Analyzing that situation, the guys didn't like me because I didn't "fit in" and wouldn't do my work at "their" speed. What it really boiled down to, I had a higher commitment level than they did, and it made them look bad. It was not my intention, but it was now my problem. I had a decision to make. Do I slow my roll, try to fit in, and go 20 miles per hour? Or do I continue my work and let them deal with their own insecurities and mediocre work ethic?

I decided to be true to who I was and continued to work hard at being a good gang cop. I was actually motivated by my critics, and that's what they were on a regular basis, my critics. In the middle of this private war with other members of this unit, a strange thing happened. I kept working to get better and made good arrests, even helping other people with their cases.

Then it happened. The backbiting and criticism stopped. To continue the criticism would shine the light on the pettiness and negative energy that was being thrown my way. I shut them down by using the very same work that got them started on me to begin with. I didn't set out to do that and didn't really know how to do that, but it happened.

I learned a valuable lesson. Some people won't like you for whatever reason they may have. If it comes down to making someone "look bad" and your intentions are honorable, you just want to be good at what you do. Keep doing what you do and at the level you are doing it, and make yourself better. You only need a few key supporters in life, not everyone.

As I look back on my career and my life, it's amazing the number of detractors that gave me the motivation to become good at what I was doing. A big "thank you" to all the haters out there.

Your Career Is Part of Your Life ... Not the Other Way Around

Life is a series of phases. School, dating, work, a bill, a car. They are all phases and parts of your life.

In law enforcement, it's the same, but it's easy for many of us to get carried away with "the job." We devote so much time and make so many sacrifices our job truly becomes our identity and our master status. When we wake up in the morning, that's who we are and what we look forward to. When we go to bed at night, it might be our last thought of, who we are, and what we accomplished that day.

The problem happens when the job becomes your whole life. A law enforcement career can be so unique and unpredictable that we tend to have phases within the phase of our career; different assignments, different partners, different ranks, and specific incidents.

Even with all of those separate phases over the course of a 10, 20, or 30-year career, they are just a part of your life. Not the other way around.

As I was getting close to retirement, people asked, "How are you going to function not being a member of the LAPD?" Most of the people asking knew me only as a cop and couldn't see me otherwise. They didn't realize; like all of us, I have other dimensions to my psyche other than being a cop.

Don't put all of your eggs in one basket. Mentally and emotionally speaking, how do you carry your eggs if your basket breaks? As Mike Tyson stated, "Everyone has a plan until they get punched in the face."

The law enforcement career can be a tantalizing seductress who takes away your desire for anything else. That's where the danger is; what happens if your seductress deceives you or, worse yet, totally abandons you?

Over the course of a 25-year career, the job at times may disappoint, discourage, and dishearten you. Put things in perspective and remember that these certain phases are part of a larger phase that comprises your life. There is life beyond your career.

There might be family, good friends, and loved ones, hobbies, and other skills you're involved in, the music you love to hear, and the trips you need to take. There are more phases and dimensions to your life. People that know you will still like and support you whether in law enforcement or not. That's how "normal" people function on an everyday basis, and they're not connected to law enforcement in any way. However, they will never understand how amazing your "seductress" made you feel when the times were good.

Even if she does walk out on you, she can't take your memories with her.

Anyone Can Be Strong When There Are Cheers and Support ... The True Test Is in Your Solitude.

Like a lot of people, I play around on Facebook. I have a lot of Facebook friends, about 500+. I maintain a Gang Cop Page and also belong to a few "law enforcement only" pages. I can interact and communicate with a lot of people and also see what they post.

I think that Facebook had created a few "types" that didn't seem to be around before it became popular. Before Facebook, people had to call, email, send a letter, or go and find someone to communicate with. Now it's just a matter of turning on your computer and putting your thoughts out there.

I really notice some "interesting" personalities on the "law enforcement only" page. I'm sure that even with law enforcement officers, there is a persona for Facebook and a different persona when that officer is actually working and facing real-life situations, not just posturing to puff up an image for the peer group.

Some officers write posts that anger the other members. Some write posts to create controversy, to gain support during a tough situation, or to brag about their assignment, their agency, or the case they just made. The response is immediate and can become addicting if you depend on the response of other people.

I post items on a daily basis, but my postings are quotes made to promote thoughts or information regarding officer safety and training issues important to other officers. I've been doing this for a few years, and it helps to keep me current and relevant with the training I provide to law enforcement.

Sometimes I read an item and the responses and think to myself, 'What would they do if Facebook didn't exist?' What if his or her thoughts didn't produce an immediate response from anyone? What did people do for recognition before Facebook?

The answer is that most of us did nothing. You learned to get what you needed as recognition from within yourself, or you learned to go without it. It's great to have support from the people close to you, but what if your issue is something that you'd rather not share? What if it's a situation or a problem that you'd rather not bother others about? I know for me, I'd rather not have people worrying about me, so I kept my mouth shut about a lot of things bothering me.

According to many experts, keeping things that bother you to yourself may not have been the ideal thing to do, but it did teach me to try and work things out mentally and emotionally on my own. It taught me not to fear being alone.

I was having a nice talk with my 17-year-old grandson one day, and I told him that one of the greatest fears people have is being alone. Some people just need to have contact and be around others. You see it in line at the market, you see it while working out at the gym, and you see it at a bar or restaurant. People are more comfortable when they feel connected, so that's why a stranger will talk to you when you're minding your own business.

You can go on Facebook and say things to gain support and cheers from your fellow professionals. You can make bold statements and feel the roar of the Facebook crowd behind you. You can also gain instant sympathy and consolation when you are in the dumps. You can get a reaction from many people.

I told my grandson if he can learn to be alone and be comfortable with it, that by itself will put him ahead of a lot of people and help him through life.

Anybody can act and talk big when the cheers and support are there. It's how you are when you're alone, and no one is around. Unfortunately, that is when some people face their darkest hour. People will still love you. People will still care about and respect you. People will even forgive you because no one is perfect. Be comfortable enough in your own skin to guide yourself through the darkness when you are alone in your solitude.

Being alone is when you can actually be at your strongest.

Everyone Walks Their Own Jungle.

When talking to officers about their personal lives, I offer a scenario; an officer goes home, and he's a little uptight about something that may have happened at work and about his job in general.

I act like I am that officer and go into a rant like he might do when he gets home to his family. The officer says, "You don't understand. I walk the jungle every day. You don't know what it's like.' He stomps around, opening and closing his hands while he walks. "You don't understand."

I then tell the crowd that everyone may have their own jungle that they walk every day. His daughter may have cheerleading tryouts, his son might have a book report due, and his wife might have 20 pounds she's trying to drop. Those are the "jungles" that each of them is walking through. You may have a challenging job sprinkled with high-pressure situations and the occasional life-or-death decision thrown in. Unless you respect the issues your family and loved ones face, it's really not fair to expect them to emotionally drop everything in their lives the moment you growl a little.

You might be loved, cherished, and respected by your family and those close to you. But if that is a one-way street for them, don't be surprised if people begin to lose interest in you. As much as they may care, their world can't be all about you all of the time. We know in law enforcement that those life-or-death situations do occur and that we see the disgusting side of human beings up close and personal. The other side of this issue is that we have voluntarily taken on this career, knowing full well the type of ugliness and injustice that may lie ahead for us.

I did not share the unpleasant side of the job very often with family and friends. I tried to shoulder much of it on my own and not try to alarm or make people worry about me. That's just me.

The way social media is used nowadays, people, including cops, can get accustomed to having instant attention thrown at them. Social media encourages opening up and talking about what's going on in your day-to-day life. Some people have learned to thrive on that.

Let's get back to my point. Most of you do very important and demanding work. Even so, you need to show concern and give attention to your loved ones when you can. To me, that is you showing your strength and encouraging those you care about to care more about you.

I'm not saying don't share or confide in others. Just try to avoid walking in the house when you get home and proclaim, "Everybody stops what you're doing. Have I told you lately that I walk the jungle?"

Everyone has their own jungle, and some of them are

bigger and scarier to them than yours is to you.

We All Have an Ugly Little Clown Inside of Us. Stop Him from Sending You Those Ugly Messages.

Many years ago, I was going through a very serious personnel investigation, and I was transferred out of my assignment and put on "restricted" duty. In this case, "restricted" meant not having any contact with the public.

Not being able to do the job I loved really pissed me off. It didn't help that during the investigation, Internal Affairs investigators were playing games and trying to do things to upset me even more. That's a whole other book for another time.

I suddenly contracted a serious case of Vertigo. It was so bad at times that I couldn't drive a car, much less walk across a residential street. I went for a series of medical tests to see if my Vertigo was due to some physical condition I had acquired. The medical test results were negative, so I was ordered to see a psychiatrist to determine if it was mental. I was "ordered" because it was considered a job-related ailment, and I basically had no choice.

So, I reluctantly went to see this psychiatrist who I believe was of Korean descent and spoke kind of broken English. You could tell that English was his second language, and I was wondering how he was going to help me.

He had me explain my situation with the personnel investigation and my job, which I did. He listened to me go on for a few minutes and then said, "You are suffering from suppressed anger."

"Okay, what does that mean?"

He went on, "You walk around mad most of the time. You have a little voice inside you that keeps saying bad things to keep you mad. You give yourself bad messages."

To me, thinking that made sense, I asked him, "How do I stop?"

He then said, "When you feel yourself sending you bad messages, you say 'stop'!" As he was saying this, he took the palm of his right hand and whacked himself on the right side of his head as if trying to jar his brain.

He further went on to say, "You learn to catch yourself sending those bad messages. It's like having a bad little person living inside you, and you learn to shut them up."

He was right. And I didn't have a clue that I was doing that to myself.

A good example of this would be if you were driving home and, for whatever reason, you anticipated some type of argument when you got there. On the way, you would be prepping yourself with your position of the dispute, and by the time you hit your front door, you're "ready to rumble."

As you walk in the door, your spouse approaches and says, "Hi, Hun. How was your day?" Then you get a kiss on the cheek. You stand there dumbfounded because you are ready for war, and there is no war. There is only what that little evil guy in your head has set you up for.

Usually, that's when you get comments like, "Are you okay? What's bugging you?" I worked on realizing that, and to this day, I still have to whack myself on the side of my head every once in a while, and say, "Knock it off."

I am fascinated and not creeped out by clowns like a lot of people are. The evil little voice inside me is my ugly little clown.

We all have disputes, arguments, and disagreements. That ugly little clown inside me seems to get busy when there is not much going on, or when there is, he doesn't know when to shut up. I needed to learn that.

Like with any toxic person, you need to control that relationship so that it doesn't wear you down and run you into the ground.

Get to know that little voice inside you and shut him up

when you have to. Only you can control that …

If You're No Good to Yourself, You're No Good to Anyone Else

Some of the best people I know are "givers." It is their nature to put everyone ahead of them and to serve others. With those types of people, it goes beyond just taking care of their family and loved ones. It is the fabric of who they are.

The problem is that most people aren't that way. Even though I don't believe most people are evil, I think many of them are "takers."

As parents, we tend to make our children takers because we want them to have happy, fulfilling lives. We should try and transition them into being givers themselves. If they grow to be takers their whole lives, what will happen when they become parents?

But the givers I know seem to always be giving. They give at home, they give at work, and they give in their relationships. They give, give, give, and give.

They have to take care of everyone and make sure that they cross the T's and dot the I's. They carry the heaviest weight and only eat after everyone else has been served.

"Givers" have to be admired because they are also the strongest people. That's why they are givers in the first place because they can handle their business and reach in to help out other people with theirs.

If you are a "giver," you might be saying right about now, "So what if I am? What business is it of yours? There are worse things I can be."

You are right. But being that you have volunteered to live your life as a "giver," there are a couple of things you should think of.

First off, you are probably appreciated more than you realize. You don't do what you do for cheers, pats on the back, or accolades. You do it out of a sense of duty. You are a caring soul who won't rest until everything is fine.

Sometimes it's hard for people's appreciation to keep up with your actions, but you are fully appreciated.

Secondly, even though you live your life doing good things for others, if something goes wrong with you, you are basically worthless to others. That's a very harsh statement to make, but if you can't even carry your own weight, how will you be yourself and take care of everyone else? You won't.

You may still be loved and admired, but you won't be able to satisfy the most important person in your life ... you.

My message is that you have to take care of yourself. You have to be a little selfish and do things that you enjoy for yourself. It might be meeting up with an old friend, reading a good book, or getting to that 12-noon yoga class. You need to reward yourself, especially if no one else is really rewarding you or making it their priority.

Do this like you've done most things in your life, by yourself, on your own, and without anyone needing to tell you to do it. But do this for yourself.

Like a powerful racecar in a 500-mile race, you need to constantly be maintaining your car (you). You need to monitor your mental, emotional, and physical levels in order to finish the race and finish it strong.

The life of a "superhero" isn't easy, or else everybody would be one. You don't see Superman adding kryptonite to his nachos because even though he is "super," he still has to take care of himself.

If you're no good to yourself, you might not be good to anyone else ... and you wouldn't want that.

The most important person affecting your morale is you.

We once had a Chief of Police who was not very popular with the troops. One day, he was at a briefing for the Department's SWAT officers, and one of the officers asked him, "Chief, what are you going to do about the morale problem in the Department?"

The Chief replied, "I'm not going to do anything about it. Morale isn't my problem; it's your problem."

Needless to say, this pissed off many of the officers. The word quickly spread throughout the Department of what the Chief had said to the SWAT officers. When I first heard it, I was kind of pissed, also. But as I thought about it, my mind started to change. Here's why …

If you are having a hard time at work for whatever reason, that can tend to work at you, at your attitude, at your motivation, and at your energy level. It can wear you down. But whatever is going on with your partner, in your unit or at your precinct or division, if you expect the Chief of Police to come to you, pat you on the head, hug you, and make you feel all better, that's not going to happen. You need to try and work it out yourself.

During the early 2000s, the morale in our Department was not great, and many officers were leaving for greener pastures. The morale in the Department was bad, but the morale in the 12-person surveillance/gang unit I was supervising was solid.

Despite what was going on with the rest of the Department, I chose to have us focus on being successful at what we were responsible for doing, locating and apprehending gang members wanted for violent crimes committed in the city of Los Angeles.

We focused and prioritized the things we had control over and pushed aside other issues that didn't affect us and had no bearing on what we did. With each of our successes, we got better and better as a unit at keeping our focus on our "prize."

As the supervisor in charge of the unit, I chose to try and avoid all of the negativity and work at being successful. It worked for my last 13 years on the job. We, as a unit, chose to stay away from the negativity.

If a squad of officers can do that, certainly you can do that for yourself.

Fight the negativity and find some success.

About the Author

Tony Moreno was born and raised in Los Angeles and became a Los Angeles police officer in 1975, spending 32 years in the Department and retiring as a Detective Supervisor in 2007.

During his career, Tony worked a variety of assignments but found his niche working in street gangs, which he successfully did for 20 of those 32 years. He established himself as one of the nation's foremost experts on street gangs and has provided formal training on gangs and related law enforcement subjects for over 35 years.

He is best known as the original "Pacman" from working gangs in South/Central Los Angeles for five years, from 1982 through 1986. During that time, he drove his trademark yellow Plymouth Fury police vehicle. His well-known nickname and yellow Plymouth were later used in the storyline of the classic gang movie "Colors."

Tony has written five other books, 'Lessons from A Gang Cop", "Spinach for the Everyday Warrior," "Cops in America Dealing with the Ferguson Effect," "Pac Man Life" and "Cop Spirit."

He is on the Advisory Board for the California Gang Investigator's Association (CGIA) and the International Latino Gang Investigator's Association (ILGIA).

Tony has two sons in law enforcement and, understanding how important our young people are to our society, has volunteered to coach youth sports for over 20 years.

Find out more about Tony Moreno at
www.gangcop.com.